From

Wimp to Warrior

By: Barbara Pillitteri
With: Susan Karas

xulon
PRESS

From Wimp to Warrior
by Barbara A. Pillitteri

Printed in the United States of America

ISBN 9781625092458

www.xulonpress.com

Table of Contents

About The Author

Barbara Pillitteri is the mother of five children, twelve grand-children, and one great grandchild. She was married to her first husband, Tom, for twenty-five years, and now twelve years to her present husband, Frank.

In addition to serving as elders at, Village of Faith Church, in Farmingville, New York, Barbara and Frank head the prayer ministry on Monday nights and share their great passion for the Word, praying for the needs of others. They expect and see mighty miracles on a regular basis.

Barbara has been the director of the Long Island Bible School for the past eight years. She is an anointed teacher with a great desire to pass on God's Word to His children, so they can walk in greater victory.

Chapter One

Where Are You God?

☩

*You will call, and the Lord will answer; you will cry for help, and
He will say: Here I am.*
(Isaiah 58:9 NIV)

There I was, pleading and begging, crying out for His help.
Where are you God? I was only twenty-five, with five children, trapped in a miserable marriage. Talks with my husband, Tom,
got me nowhere.

"You and the children have a roof over your head and food to
eat. Don't you? What more do you want?"

That was easy; I wanted my husband back, the sweet one, the
guy who asked me to share his life forever. I wanted his love, a
warm smile, and most definitely a hug. But it didn't come. *God
where is the man I married?*

We looked like a perfect family, but there was a lot of tension in
our home. All I could do was hope things would get better because I
didn't believe in divorce. We both knew our marriage wasn't what it
should be and agreed to try harder. That's when I got pregnant with
twins! Two more beautiful daughters, but nothing changed and two
years later I was pregnant again.

Instead of the children drawing us closer we grew further
apart. Tom became controlling, belligerent, and moody. Filled with

resentment and bitterness, I was going tit-for-tat over everything, and began to hate him... then myself, for who I'd become. What happened to me? I was always the peacemaker.

As the children grew into teenagers, they started to act out, make wrong decisions, and hang around with undesirable friends. I was at my wits end. My family was falling apart and I didn't know how to stop it. There was no one to confide in because Tom didn't like me to socialize, so it was easier to stay home than deal with the repercussions of going against him.

Wound tight and ready to snap I started to think of ways to escape the tension. Anything to numb the pain of the situation. I tried my husband's valium, only that didn't help; I wasted the entire day slumped like a "Valley Doll" across the sofa. Then, I figured maybe a drink would work, so I had one a half hour before Tom was due home, just to calm my nerves. But becoming an alcoholic wasn't the answer either, so I stopped that, too. Thoughts of suicide crossed my mind, but how could I leave my children without a mother? *What am I going to do? God, please help me!*

The kids and I were being destroyed, slowly... a little more each day. There was no choice left. Leaving Tom was the only answer. I called my sister-in-law, Nina, to ask her how she went about getting her divorce. To my surprise, Nina already knew how desperate I felt. She'd written a letter to me weeks before to offer her help, but never mailed it.

"Do you want me to read it to you?"

"Yes," I sobbed.

It began by saying she knew Tom and I were having difficulty in our marriage, that she could see how scared and alone I was. She went on to pose a question. If you were on a road and lost, what would you do to find your way? Wouldn't you ask someone who knew; someone who had a map or directions for you?

By then I was sobbing even more and just wanted to know what to do.

"The Bible is that map, Barbara," she said. Then, she told me her Pastor did marriage counseling and asked if I'd like an appointment. My pain was so great, without hesitation, I said yes.

Although I always had a basic faith, as a child I'd only gone to church with the neighbors. My parents were not supportive of the church environment, but they did allow my sister and me to go, when we'd asked. Now, with desperation in my heart, I hoped Nina's Pastor would offer something to hold on to.

A few days later, I met with the Pastor. He told me all about having a personal relationship with the Lord. He spoke about faith, and then led me in prayer to receive Jesus into my heart. But when I left his office my shoulders were slumped and I wondered how any of this was going to help. The Pastor had instructed me to read certain scriptures, so I started with that. Whatever it took, I was willing and obedient; anything to stop the pain.

Wednesday mornings, I attended his Bible study. When the first class was about disappointments and how they led to bitterness, I knew I was in the right place. From then on, each meeting was a booster shot to carry me through the week.

For days at a time I was encouraged, making wonderful progress. Then, for no apparent reason I would fall back into discouragement and defeat again. *Why, Lord, this isn't right?*

At the very next Bible study, the Pastor's wife suggested we read Proverbs every day, one chapter for that day of the month. Each time I reached chapter twenty-four, verse ten spoke to me, *if you faint in the day of adversity your strength is small."* That was it! I'm a wimp… up one day and down the next.

After several months of reading and re-reading Proverbs 24:10 and hearing only condemnation in the words, the Lord brought my attention to verse five in that same chapter. It was as if the words popped right off the page, *Knowledge increases strength.*

With strength I could hold onto my victory. That was the answer! The only way to increase strength was by continuing to read the Bible and learn God's Word. If I was going to be strong, I needed His knowledge. It was my moment of clarity! I finally understood. And so began my pursuit for His knowledge and my journey from despair to triumph, "from Wimp to Warrior."

Chapter Two

His Perfect Will

☩

Do not conform any longer to the pattern of this world, but be trans-
formed by the renewing of your mind. Then you will be able to test
and approve what God's will is – His good, pleasing, and perfect will.
(Romans 12:2 NIV)

Eager to learn more, I dug into the Bible. *All right, God, who
are You?* As I read and studied it became apparent that God's
character was not at all like the father I grew up with, strict and
unreasonable, and rarely spoke a word of encouragement. No, the
Bible tells us our Heavenly Father is... *the Rock, His works are perfect, and all His ways are just. A faithful God who does no wrong,
upright and just is He* (Deuteronomy 32:4-5 NIV). Page after page,
scripture after scripture, a new image began to form. God is full of
love, compassion, mercy, and wisdom.

I tried to be more like my heavenly Father and walk away, but
before I knew it Tom had provoked me into another fight. There I
was, going tit-for-tat with him again. I went into the bedroom and
dropped to my knees, tears rolling. *How am I supposed to continue
in this marriage God, I hate him!* The minute the words were out,
my face burned with shame; I wasn't acting anything at all like
Jesus. My thoughts shifted to the pain he must have endured that
night in the garden before going to the cross. His agony was much

greater than mine. Instead of railing, He asked the Father, *"take this cup from me."* And even as He sweat great drops of blood He'd said, *"nevertheless, Father, Your will not mine."* If He could withstand that, then I could certainly find the strength to put up with an unhappy marriage. Kneeling there on the bedroom floor I surrendered. "Nevertheless, Father, Your will not mine."

Along with my surrender came a flood of tears. "Okay, God, I can't do it, so I'm just going to let You do it for me." I walked out of that bedroom that night determined to stop falling into the same old trap. From then on, through every confrontation, I prayed for the strength to hold back ugly retorts. And I finally succeeded! That just about blew his mind, but not enough to change anything. In fact, with all my trying to do the right thing, the situation got worse instead of better, and Tom eventually initiated divorce proceedings.

Learning who God is and all of His promises became my strength during those troubled times. Just as my sister-in-law had told me, the Bible was the map which helped me to walk through it all, moving me another step along the path from wimp to warrior.

Chapter Three

Simple, Heartfelt Words

☩

*Do not be like them, for your Father knows what you need before
you ask Him. This then, is how to pray.
(Matthew 6: 8-9 NIV)*

There were many days I wanted to crawl into bed with the covers over my head, but instead I cried out to the Lord with simple, heartfelt words; my prayer. In time, the Lord led me to a deeper prayer life and I was able to make "The Lord's Prayer" more personal. Oh, we still had simple conversations, but understanding and being able to personalize the prayer Jesus taught the disciples brought me so much further on my walk with him.

Our Father who art in Heaven. Our Father is the Creator, and I am His child. He knows me personally; saves me from the powers of darkness, and loves me with an everlasting love. That's why I can trust Him to answer my prayers, protect, and guide me. *"For I know the plans I have for you," declares the Lord, "plans to prosper you and not harm you, plans to give you hope and a future"* (Jeremiah 29:11 NIV). God is faithful and His Word is true, so I can believe in His wonderful plans for me.

Hallowed be Thy name. Just like the psalmist David, I ask the Lord to help me to follow in His holy steps. *Teach me your way, O Lord, and I will walk in your truth; give me an undivided heart, that I may fear your name* (Psalm 86:11 NIV). Several years back, WWJD bracelets were big. You don't see them around much anymore, but I remember the message: *What Would Jesus Do?* The question speaks about character... thoughts, actions, and words. Whether I'm around others or all alone, my Father sees my character. When I act according to God's word it pleases Him and releases His blessings to me.

Thy Kingdom come, Thy will be done, on earth as it is in heaven. The apostle Paul explained the kingdom of God as righteousness, peace, and joy. And in Luke 17:21 it says *The Kingdom of God is within you.* His will is that I abide in His Word, and that it be done on earth... everywhere... in my life, home, and family. Living in His perfect will assures me of a life filled with peace, joy, and health.

Give us this day our daily bread. When I hear this, I think, thank you for supplying daily bread for my body and the bread of Your Word to feed my soul. I ask God to help me cast my care on Him. *So do not worry, saying, 'What shall we eat?' or 'What shall we drink?' or 'What shall we wear?' For the pagans run after all these things and your heavenly Father knows that you need them* (Matthew 6:31-32 NIV). This scripture assures me there is no need for concern. He will supply all my needs.

Forgive us our sins, as we forgive others. How can I be right with God and feel blessed if I am living with sin? I can't, so I pray to be open and honest, hiding nothing as I confess to Him. *If we confess our sins, He is faithful and just and will forgive us our sins and purify us from all unrighteousness* (1 John 1:9 NIV). What a blessing! This scripture gives me the assurance of forgiveness. And when He forgives me I learn to forgive others.

I wanted my relationship right with God, but I was so angry with my husband, I didn't think it was possible to forgive him. Over and over I forgave Tom, but one day I'd just about had all I could take. With my heart full of ugly bitterness, I ran into my room and railed at the Lord, "I hate him; I keep forgiving and he keeps hurting me. I can't forgive him again" *Forgive us our sins, as we forgive others* immediately came to mind and I changed my plea, "Lord, I can't forgive him, so until I can, please forgive him through me."

Lead us not into temptation but deliver us from evil. Temptation is a trap. *Watch and pray so that you will not fall into temptation* (Matthew 26:41 NIV). And how was I going to do that, I wondered? Provoking me had become a game to Tom. Again and again, I took the bait he dangled before me. The temptation was to jump on him, retaliate, yell and hurt back. "Lord, help me see the snares. Give me discernment and wisdom and the strength to resist." 2 Thessalonians 3:3 says: *"The Lord is faithful, and He will strengthen and protect us from evil…"* The next time he tried to rile me, I remembered that scripture and God spoke to my heart… *walk away.* He supplied me with the fortitude to do just that, and sure enough, delivered me from the "evil" of another nasty fight.

Yours is the kingdom, the power, and the glory forever. All I can do is drop to my knees and give thanks. Thank You, Lord, that You have provided my salvation, rescued me out of the kingdom of darkness and into the kingdom of Your dear Son. I know that in my own strength I can do nothing, so I give you the glory and honor for everything You have done, for me and through me.

It's *His* power and might that brings us into greater victory. Praise the Lord! Take this new understanding of the Lord's Prayer and make it personal for you. Simply talk to God and don't forget to listen for His voice. That's what I did and it's taken me another step on the journey from wimp to warrior.

Chapter Four

Ask What You Will

☩

Be anxious for nothing, but in prayer and petition, with present
your requests to God.
(Philippians 4:6 NIV)

My life began to change as I leaned on the Lord. I didn't know how or when it happened, but the darkness and emotional despair that once consumed me was slowly replaced by hope. Instead of wallowing in bitterness and anger, I turned to God in prayer and trusted that my uncomfortable situations were only temporary and everything would soon improve.

I learned that when we pray, if we ask with the right attitude, one of trust and confidence, we will receive what we ask for. *And if we know that He hears us—whatever we ask—we know that we have what we asked of him* (1 John 5:14 NIV). This is a faith principle. In other words, you can have whatever you say; it always works. And don't forget, it works the other way as well. If you say negative things, then that's what will come to pass. We should be humble and reverent towards God. You see, there are always two fundamental ends for what God wants to accomplish – everything must be for His glory and our good. Prayers must have that same purpose – for His glory and for the good of those we pray for.

Ask in His name. *You may ask me for anything in my name, and I will do it* (John 14:14 NIV). We need to remember that name equals nature, so our prayers must always be motivated by love, the nature of God.

Pray and remain steadfast. Have faith that God will answer your prayers. Faith filled prayer is speaking God's Word. . . words He has already spoken. Then, just believe. That's all there is to faith! Don't keep talking about the problem. Not to God, or people. Instead, focus on the answer. Declare scripture over it. God, your word says, *I tell you the truth, If anyone says to this mountain, 'Go, throw yourself in the sea,' and does not doubt in his heart, but believes that what he says will happen, it will be done for him* (Mark 11:22-23 NIV). I stood on that promise and it wasn't long before I saw it manifest in my life. God is always true to His word.

Get the right things in your heart—wrong thinking will bring wrong believing. Every word that passes your lips is a seed being planted in your own heart. God is never too busy to hear our prayers. Don't be shy about your requests. As His children we are encouraged to ask for anything we have need of. Simply pray and remain in faith that God not only hears, but answers.

As a mother, it was a relief to know that my prayers were out there working to keep my children under divine protection. But some nights were simply harder than others. One particular evening tested my faith more than usual. I'd been exceptionally worried about my son and couldn't shake the feeling that something was very wrong. So I kept praying, harder and harder until he finally came home. There'd been an accident. It was rainy and the roads were slick. He'd swerved on a wide curve and crashed head on with another car.

"Mom, I know you were praying for me," he said, and rolled up his pant legs for me to see. "My car was totaled, but I walked away with only these scratches."

"Praise God," I cried out, looking in wonder at his scraped knees. The Lord was faithful to answer my prayer.

Armed with a powerful prayer life and a constant heart of gratitude, I was now firmly on my way from wimp to warrior.

Chapter Five

Praise is Powerful

☩

Now, our God, we give you thanks, and praise your glorious name.
(1 Chronicles 29:13 NIV)

Did you know praise is simply expressing our gratitude to God? Praise glorifies the name of God, and is another way of thanking Him for all He has done. In Psalm 100:4 we are told, *Enter his gates with thanksgiving, and his courts with praise; give thanks to him and Praise his name.* Praise offers protection. In fact, the original meaning for the word "courts" is enclosed yard. When I had young children we fenced in our yard so they couldn't get out and nothing could get in to harm them. Just like a parent, God will protect us from the enemy. Next time you praise Him, picture yourself in that safe place and remember, your heavenly Father's right there guarding the gate.

Praise shelters us from harm and lifts us up. According to scripture, praise frees us from heaviness and bestows *...a garment of praise instead of a spirit of despair* (Isaiah 61:3 NIV). God always does His part, but He expects us to do ours. When we're down, we need to put on that "garment of praise" by expressing our thanks and admiration. Isn't that what we do in church, revere Him with extended hands? It may feel awkward at first, but soon enough, praising God openly will become as natural as taking a breath. And we are to praise God not only in the good times, but also in the bad.

Each time I chose going to church to praise God over staying home to wallow in self-pity, the result was amazing. As hard as it was to believe, I left strengthened and encouraged every single time. David, the Psalmist, wrote… *you fill me with joy in your presence* (Psalm 16:11 NIV). The joy of the Lord is our strength. In His presence we will always know that kind of joy.

I remember a particular church service where we had a blackout. Everyone was content to sit there in the dark, praising God. I became so filled with the spirit, I actually felt intoxicated. Laughter bubbled up in me the whole way home, until I walked through the door. It was less than a minute before Tom started to berate me, each word a poison dart, but it didn't rattle me. No tit-for-tat this time! Those nasty darts bounced right off of me; it was as though I had a shield of protection. Just another reason for more praise!

Sometimes praise is sacrificial … *Let us continually offer to God a sacrifice of praise…* (Hebrews 13:15 NIV). There are times I'm simply not in the mood to thank Him, but I do it anyway. The Lord is worthy of blessing and no matter how I feel at the moment I'm always happy I did the right thing.

Our praise is a weapon. In the spiritual realm, our fight is not against flesh and blood but against powers, principalities, and rulers of the darkness. Praise is an all out attack that stops the enemy cold and we can dispel those worrisome or distressing thoughts with the Word. At a time when I was fighting depression and fear I wrote a scripture on an index card and kept it on my night stand, *But those who hope in the Lord will renew their strength. They will soar on wings like eagles; they will run and not grow weary, they will walk and not be faint* (Isaiah 40:31 NIV). When I'd read those words out loud every morning the weariness lifted and I was ready to soar like the eagles. Is there something you can think of to praise God for? What kind of start do you think that would give your day?

Paul and Silas knew very well the benefits of praise. They had been flogged, chained, and thrown in prison. It was a dark time for them yet they didn't cower in fear in their cell. *About midnight Paul and Silas were praying and singing hymns to God, and the other prisoners were listening to them. Suddenly there was such a violent earthquake that the foundations of the prison were shaken. At once all the prison doors flew open, and everybody's chains came loose* (Acts 16:25-26). That's what I call results!

It's clear, praise is a powerful weapon. If we remain faithful, praising the Lord in good times and bad, continuing on the path from wimp to warrior, our wonderful and mighty Lord will surely bring us to greater victory.

Chapter Six

Power Under Restraint

☦

Trust in the Lord with all your heart and lean not on your own understanding; in all your ways submit to him, and he will make your paths straight.
(Proverbs 3:5-6 NIV)

As I continued my journey from wimp to warrior, the Lord taught me the importance of submission. I had always disliked that word because I thought it meant to give in or let someone get the upper hand, but that wasn't it at all. Submission is not weakness, it's power under restraint. Simply put, submission is becoming obedient to the Lord. When I yielded my will to His, suddenly the word was less threatening. What a relief to realize we don't have to carry everything on our shoulders. God will do it for us – and He'll do it better, too.

Humility goes hand in hand with submission. We cannot or will not submit without first being humble. It's arrogant and prideful to depend on ourselves rather than God. James 4:6-7 lays it out clearly. *God opposes the proud by gives grace to the humble.* It's not always easy, but the reward is great. When we're willing to be obedient to God, life is not only fulfilling, but orderly, and peaceful as well. Sure, there'll be seasons of trial and stress, but because we're submitting to God, we can walk through those seasons knowing that He'll see us through to a better place each and every time.

When I first heard, "submit," I cried out, "Lord, how can I submit to the authority of others when all they've ever done is hurt me?" But the Word of God is clear. . . we need to make the choice to submit in *every* area of our lives.

Apply it to my marriage, too? No, I thought, that can't be right. Submit to the man who heaped abuse on me, wasn't even a believer, and never so much as opened the Bible. Submit anyway? It was absurd! But there it was, in Ephesians 5:22: *Wives, submit to your husbands as to the Lord. For the husband is the head of the wife as Christ is the head of the church, his body, of which he is the Savior. Now as the church submits to Christ, so also wives should submit to their husbands in everything.* I didn't like it one bit, but if God wanted me to submit to my husband I would. Although, one of the few times I did take exception to that was when Tom asked me to get on the phone and lie to an insurance agent. He wasn't too happy and his temper did flare, but he finally realized I wouldn't go against God's Word, no matter what.

The Word also tells us to submit to one another. *Submit to one another out of reverence for Christ* (Ephesians 5:21 NIV). If we respect God, we need to respect one another. I thought about my family and friends, and the times there was discord between us. Back then I would have been caught up in the drama. Not anymore. How different life would be if everyone realized the benefit of submission. Living in harmony with others demonstrates the love of Christ to the world around us. It didn't take much, but with every little effort like holding my tongue or letting the other person be right, I began to see the blessing of submission.

Scripture even covers the workplace. *Submit yourselves to your masters (employers) with all respect, not only to those who are good and considerate, but also to those who are harsh*

(1 Peter 2:18 NIV). I'm sure we can all relate to the crabby boss or the supervisor who never gets to work on time, but expects you to be there. That's God's business, ours is to obey the Word and be in submission to the authority above us.

As I continued to read the Word, I realized submission is more than just obedience to the Lord, it has a greater purpose. We submit to stay in agreement. *Again I tell you that if two of you on earth agree about anything you ask for, it will be done for you by my Father in heaven* (Matthew 18:19 NIV). When we agree, and abide in His Word, we can ask what we will.

We submit to demonstrate love. *By this all men will know you are my disciples, if you love one another* (John 13:35 NIV). Walking in love keeps us in harmony with our Lord and with others.

We submit to stay in peace. *Let the peace of Christ rule in your hearts, since as members of one body you were called to peace* (Colossians 3:15 NIV).

God's Word clearly shows us submitting is not just being a "yes man;" it's an awesome tool, which brings strength, peace, and the grace of God into our lives. By accepting that fact, I was now another step closer on my journey from wimp to warrior.

Chapter Seven

When Trials Come

✠

God is our refuge and strength, an ever-present help in trouble.
(Psalm 46:1 NIV)

After making the choice to follow Christ, I thought life would be different, easier somehow. Not so! In fact, 1 Peter 4:12 tells us *not to be surprised* when trials come. We're not exempt from troubles just because we have Christ as our Savior, but what we do have is the faithful promise of God that everything will be used for our good and His glory. Once we can get that point we'll begin to see things differently.

Did you know trials aren't sent by our heavenly Father? They come from outside forces, people, and circumstances. God isn't to blame for tragedies, accidents, or illness. Sometimes we create our own circumstances, and other times, satan gets the credit for those things. His feeble attempts to discourage and turn us against God will never work. They're lies! God sent His only Son to take our suffering, so that we may have life and have it more abundantly. What does that say? Simple, we can trust God to use everything for our benefit even bad things. You see, it's at those broken times that we are the most receptive to His promptings.

One of the greatest trials I've had to face was when my son and his friends were arrested in Maryland where they'd stolen a truck, stopped for gas, and left the station without paying. The state troopers set up a barricade and when the boys were caught, one of the troopers claimed my son had tried to run him down. As a result, my son was charged with attempted murder and held for trial.

I sat in the hallway outside the courtroom and cried out, "Lord, I am weak; please help me."

"My strength is made perfect in your weakness." It was unmistakable. That scripture was delivered immediately to my heart. Confident the Lord was with me, I stood and walked into the courtroom.

To my amazement, the lawyers had asked me to participate in the jury selection that day and I (unknowingly) chose an airline pilot who was able to calculate the speed and distance my son had driven, proving the trooper's accusation mathematically impossible. The attempted murder charge was miraculously dropped!

It's not easy, but if we remember God has given us the grace to outlast any problem, we can make it through the circumstances. God will always take what the enemy meant for harm and use it to make us better and stronger.

After experiencing how God intervenes on our behalf, the sense of peace that I have is beyond understanding. I can walk away from taunting, dismiss fear, hold my head high, and all with a humble heart. I am a new creature in Christ, completely certain that no matter what the problem, every trial is temporary... just another challenge on my way from wimp to warrior.

Chapter Eight

That's Grace!

☦

Let us then approach the throne of grace with confidence,
so that we may receive mercy and find grace to help us in our
time of need.
(Hebrews 4:16 NIV)

I sn't it a comfort to know our Heavenly Father never leaves us unprotected? He equips us to endure whatever it is we're facing. Right in the midst of our struggles, He provides the wonderful gifts of grace and peace.

Grace is favor from the Lord. It actually transforms us, renews the heart, and restrains us from sin. Discouragement may try to grip you, even make you want to give up, but grace will cause you to hold on!

There's a saying, when you're down to nothing, God's up to something. That's exactly what happened, God's wonderful grace saved my life and brought me hope. It was when I finally reached my bottom that I met the pastor who led me in prayer to receive the Lord. I easily could have been an alcoholic, drug addict, or suffering from a nervous breakdown in a mental hospital. Even worse, a suicide statistic. Instead, with God's help my life started to change. That's grace!

I can look back and see how many things God has saved me from. Every time I struggled with a decision to go God's way or my way, if I humbled myself before the Lord and simply asked, I received His grace for that very situation. *God resists the proud and gives grace to the humble (James 4:6 NIV).*

Grace leads us to what we need and then God's peace keeps us there. It's not the kind of peace the world gives that comes only when everything is going good. Jesus said: *Peace I leave you; my peace I give you. I do not give to you as the world gives. Do not let your hearts be troubled and do not be afraid* (John 14:27 NIV). Do you see what this scripture is saying? It's our choice. We can let ourselves become agitated and let our emotions control us, or hold on to what the Lord has so graciously given... His peace.

Instead of dwelling on problems think about what Philippians 4:6-9 says. *Whatever is true, whatever is noble, whatever is right, whatever is pure, whatever is lovely, whatever is admirable – if anything is excellent or praiseworthy – think about such things.*

That scripture really made an impression on me. I copied it onto an index card and placed it on my refrigerator. I read it aloud and tried to substitute upsetting thoughts with things that were true, noble, and lovely. Old habits are hard to break, but I didn't give up even though Tom and the kids still set me off from time to time. It took a full month, but it finally happened; the peace of God filled my heart again, just like the last time, just like He promised.

I'm now convinced there's no battle too big. With God in my corner I can get through anything. His grace and peace have brought me another step further from wimp and closer to warrior.

Chapter Nine

Faith That Grows

✟

*Now faith is confidence in what we hope for and assurance about
what we do not see.
This is what the ancients were commended for.
(Hebrews 11:1-2 NIV)*

There are some amazing examples of faith in the Bible. Moses,
Noah and Job were all faith-filled men who put their trust in
God. However, the source of faith in the Old Testament was the law.
During that time, obedience was a matter of "have to" and "right"
was based on conscience, and conscience went right back to law. Of
course, no one could live perfectly by the law, so it became a vicious
cycle. The people sinned, God was angry, the people repented ... God
gave them another chance, and so it went. But the New Testament
changed all that.

God is constant and true, and bound to us by the new covenant
He made when Jesus was sacrificed on the cross. Therefore, we are
now persuaded by the work of the Holy Spirit. *This is the covenant I
will make with them after that time, says the Lord. I will put my laws
in their hearts, and I will write them on their minds.* (Hebrews 10:
15-16 NIV). We no longer need to hear through prophets or angels;
God promised to speak directly to our hearts, and His promises are
always yea and amen.

We have faith in His promises because we are now new creatures in Christ with a new heart and new desires. Before I was saved, I didn't think twice about doing things that were wrong before God, but once I got saved I didn't want to do those things any longer. I didn't follow God's laws because I "had to" like the Old Testament people, but because I "wanted to."

I can remember the first time I wanted to do right, when it was heavy on my heart. I'd left the grocery store and as I was loading the packages into my car I noticed a greeting card had slipped underneath the bags. I hadn't paid for that card! There was a time when I would have said, "Their mistake is my gain." Not now. I hurried right back into that store and paid the cashier. She was surprised I'd come back for such a small amount, but I quickly explained that I loved the Lord and wanted to please Him. It wasn't a matter of "have to" anymore. I wanted to!

Once I had the desire to grow in His Word, getting into a full Bible believing church helped me hear the Word. *Consequently, faith comes from hearing the message, and the message is heard through the word of Christ* (Romans 10:17 NIV). Exercising my "spiritual muscles" resulted in greater faith, like the Centurion in Luke 7:9. He was a man of authority and knew when a man of authority spoke, what he spoke was done. There was no need for further evidence to persuade him aside from the Word of Jesus. And how can we not be persuaded by the testimony of such faith? For that Centurion believed that Jesus had to only "speak the words," and his servant would be healed. And he was, that very hour!

Faith operates by speaking. When God created this world He spoke it into existence. "Let there be light." And there was light. Our words are so powerful. *Life and death are in the power of the tongue* (Proverbs 18:21 NIV). In other words, what we speak will come to pass. Are you speaking negative things that bring only death or are you lining up with God's Word and choosing life? There was a couple in my church who every time I asked, "How are you?" They always answered, "Blessed." I would get so annoyed. They weren't blessed, not with the serious financial problems they were dealing with. But they knew the power of the spoken word and God honored their faith. He delivered them from those difficulties.

In order to receive results like that we have to believe what we speak. When you truly understand this, you'll see mighty things come to pass in your lives.

Paul encouraged the early church to keep their hearts fixed on God. *Be on your guard; stand firm in the faith; be men of courage; be strong* (1 Corinthians 16:13 NIV). That's still true today. Guard your hearts! And your minds, too. Be careful and downright choosy what you put before those eyes and ears. The things we see and hear are seeds being planted in the garden of our hearts. Let only things that will produce faith grow there. Keep your garden weeded. After a plant is placed in good soil it needs sun, air and water in order to grow and thrive. Spiritually we need the same; Jesus the Son (sun), the Holy Spirit (air), and the Word (water). So keep yourself exposed to the right elements and you'll thrive.

I remember watching a Christian show on television. A man was holding a Bible and speaking. I didn't know why at the time, but I shut him off. Another time I was listening to Christian radio and the same thing happened; a man was preaching and I shut him off, too. *Why don't I want to hear this Lord? I love your Word.* A few months later, I was at a seminar where they spoke about known heretics, those who preach falsely. Both of the men I shut off were mentioned. Wow! I was a young Christian and could have easily been deceived, but the Holy Spirit guided me away from what I wasn't supposed to hear. *Thank goodness!*

Remember, great faith comes by hearing, and hearing by the Word of God. So listen, read, and don't forget to speak out those faith-filled words. Before you know it, you too will be taking another step from wimp to warrior!

Chapter Ten

Equipped With God's Wisdom

☩

So that the man of God may be thoroughly equipped for every good work.
(2 Timothy 3:17 NIV)

So what now? As my walk continued, my desire to share the Lord grew. I thought of the passage in James 1:23-24 *Anyone who listens to the word but does not do what it says is like a man who looks at his face in a mirror and after looking at himself, goes away, and immediately forgets what he looks like.*

Once we have knowledge and understanding we can apply it to our lives. Being a doer of the Word is wisdom and His wisdom is His will. Whatever it says in the Word – do it! Such a joy rises up within me when I obey what God says.

God has a purpose and a plan for each of us. So, when I felt the Lord urging me to go to my neighbor's house and tell them how Jesus had changed my life, I put down my coffee and went. As I tried to explain how simply accepting Jesus is what draws you closer to God, they became very defensive about their beliefs, but their son who was resting on the couch had heard every word I'd said. I walked out of their home thinking nothing had happened, but was still filled with joy because I knew I had been obedient to the Lord. Later, I was astounded to learn that the boy on the sofa had a brain tumor and passed away soon after my visit. God had sent me to bring the message to that child. If I hadn't gone, he would have died without knowing about Jesus. Here I was thinking that I was there for the parents! What a powerful example of what happens when we walk in the will of God.

We have to make choices on a daily basis. If we're going to act in the will of God, our decisions have to be in line with His Word, not based on our feelings. God's will is revealed by the Spirit. If we choose from a mind that has been filled and renewed with God's Word, the Spirit leads us into perfect alignment with His will. Pay attention… if there's discomfort in your "gut," stop. But if what you're doing produces peace in your heart, then move ahead. Do nothing without that peace.

I had a friend who had been a Christian for quite some time. She seemed very knowledgeable in the things of God, and we got together often. One morning she said that God told her we should go to a prayer meeting. I felt no peace about it, but what could be wrong with a prayer meeting? So I went even though it didn't feel right. When I got home the phone was ringing. It was the school. They were trying to get me all morning. My son had been injured and they needed to reach me. That was a perfect example of not choosing His will. I didn't listen to my "gut."

We have not stopped praying for you and asking God to fill you with the knowledge of His will through all spiritual wisdom and understanding (Colossians 1:9 NIV). Here, Paul tells us how important it is to be in the will of God. When you know God's will you're able to act with calm assurance.

When Tom and I were settling our divorce I wanted my lawyer to include three things that were important to me. He said it was too late to make any changes, so I found a new lawyer. This one was a Christian, which made me more comfortable sharing how the Lord had guided me to pursue the additional terms. It would cost thousands to go back to court, he told me, and if we did, I'd probably lose anyway. I was disappointed, but in my heart I heard... *stand still and see the salvation of the Lord.* And I knew the Lord would fight my battle.

Our lawyers met and Tom's insisted his client would never agree to the changes, declaring he was a very stubborn man. No matter how hard Tom and his attorney tried to persuade me to change my mind, I didn't. Wisdom waits and emotions hurry. I stood firm on what the Lord had told me instead of giving in to fear, even though it meant going back to court. It turned out that Tom changed his mind; we never went back to court. God had indeed won that battle for me!

Isn't it a comfort to know He's always there equipping and enabling us, giving us His power and all that we need to continue the journey from wimp to warrior.

Chapter Eleven

I Will Not Be Moved

☩

You will keep in perfect peace him whose mind is steadfast,
because he trusts in you.
(Isaiah 26:3 NIV)

Moving from wimp to warrior takes not only faith but a firm resolve to grow in the Word. *Steadfast.* That's what I wanted... to be steadfast.

Even in the Old Testament we see how Jehoshaphat faced a vast army, but the Lord sent him a prophecy that they were not to be afraid or discouraged, that the battle was His. Jehoshaphat was steadfast, holding onto that Word, and sure enough, against unheard of odds, they were able to defeat the mighty army. *As they began to sing and praise, the LORD set ambushes against the men of Ammon and Moab and Mount Seir who were invading Judah, and they were defeated (2 Chronicles 20:22).*

There were many scriptures like that, ones which helped me on my journey, moving me from bitterness to hopeful expectation. The Lord taught me to pray and wait expectantly – not wonder if my prayers were going to be answered. During the waiting it's easy to become afraid or discouraged. *Fear not, I am with you, be not dismayed, for I am your God, I will strengthen you, I will help you, I will hold you up (Isaiah 41:10).* That's one of my favorite scriptures, the one I turn to when I'm trying to remain steadfast in the face of adversity. What a comfort, what an encouragement. God is right there with us! *We have this hope as an anchor for the soul, firm and secure* (Hebrews 6:19). Even in the midst of a storm, just as an anchor holds that boat in place, God's promises keep us steady and stable.

Paul, who wrote most of the New Testament, was a powerful example of being steadfast. *I have fought the good fight, I have finished the race, I have kept the faith.* He wrote in

2 Timothy 4:7. What confidence, what certainty. He kept his eye on the prize and finished his course. That only came with a purpose in his heart, to be faithful to the Lord – steadfast!

The devil will do anything he can to tear down the decisions we make for Christ. He comes along and plants the wrong kind of seeds that produce weeds of wrong thinking and wrong feelings. We have to stand in faith believing the Word of God. *Make level paths for your feet and take only ways that are firm. Do not swerve to the right or the left, keep your foot from evil* (Proverbs 4:26-27 NIV). In other words, be determined and stand strong... be steadfast. When temptation comes, remember, *Submit yourselves, then, to God, resist the devil, and he will flee from you* (James 4:7 NIV). Don't be moved by the devil's schemes.

The enemy tries to weaken our resolve with fear, doubt, and worry; even sickness and disease. While I was working as a home health care nurse, the family I was assigned to all came down with the flu. All the nurses caught it; everyone except me. The old me would have said, "I'm going to catch this, too!" Thank heaven I resisted the temptation to worry and speak negative things over myself, words contrary to God's Word. I was steadfast, resisted the devil, and sure enough he fled.

Shadrach, Meshach and Abednego were three young men who were facing a fiery furnace because of their devotion to God. *Nebuchadnezzar said to them, "Is it true, Shadrach, Meshach and Abednego, that you do not serve my gods or worship the image of gold I have set up? Now when you hear the sound of the horn, flute, zither, lyre, harp, pipe and all kinds of music, if you are ready to fall down and worship the image I made, very good. But if you do not worship it, you will be thrown immediately into a blazing furnace. Then what god will be able to rescue you from my hand?" Shadrach, Meshach and Abednego replied to him, "King Nebuchadnezzar, we do not need to defend ourselves before you in this matter. If we are thrown into the blazing furnace, the God we serve is able to deliver us from it, and he will deliver us from Your Majesty's hand* (Daniel 3:14-17 NIV). They refused to fear, or bow to him. "Our God will deliver us," they declared. What confidence! They had unshakeable faith, rooted and grounded in trust for the Lord. They were steadfast!

I want that kind of faith! To stand that firm. I have a vision for myself and for all Christians alike. We shall demonstrate that we are far above the ways of the world in every area of our lives – physically, emotionally, mentally, and socially; more physically fit, emotionally stable and of sound mind. Our decisions wiser, our relationships closer and more meaningful. When we are steadfast and stay within His power and grace, we will no longer be wimps, but shall be full fledged warriors.

Chapter Twelve

Fully Persuaded

✝

No, in all these things we are more than conquerors…
(Romans 8:3-7 NIV)

As I moved along my journey of transformation the Lord blessed me with Frankie, my present husband, a man of deep faith. I love the way he prays when someone comes to him. He always asks, "What can you believe for?" Then, he stands in agreement with them. Sometimes, he'll even explain what God's Word says about their situation in order to give them a stronger basis for believing. Frankie also shares his experience of how God healed him from herniated discs, which caused severe back and leg pain.

When the doctors had said there was nothing more they could do, Frankie went to the Village of Faith Church. He had heard about how they ministered on the healing power of God. Every week, he went and stood on their prayer line to have hands laid on him and scripture spoken over him. "I guess it didn't work," he said each time he returned to his seat with the same pain. But one particular time, he went back to his seat and declared he didn't care what he felt, he was healed by the power of God. After that, Frankie took another leap of faith and stopped wearing the back support the doctors had given him. One day, when the pain was incredibly severe, he decided to put the brace back on. It was barely in place when he heard the audible voice of God. It was the first and only time, but He said, "Are you going to trust in that thing or are you going to trust in my Word?"

"Oh, Lord!" said my husband, as he pulled the support off. "I know I'm healed." Immediately, the pain left. The pain was gone for weeks and Frankie was able to work pain free. Then, on another day, he felt a sharp pain in his back again. He dropped his butcher knife and said, "In the name of Jesus, get off my back. I am healed by the stripes of Jesus." The pain left immediately. This time it was for good.

We trust in God and continue to speak His Word over ourselves and all situations. Every morning, as we sip our coffee, Frankie chooses several scriptures and we pray them out loud. This kind of praying, using God's Word, is in complete alignment with His will. *Again, I tell you that if two of you on earth agree about anything you ask, it will be done for you by my Father in heaven* (Matthew 18:19 NIV). Agreement is important and powerful.

I remember a time, Frank and I were invited to go to our daughters for a family barbecue. Tom would be there and Frank felt leery about going. After some discussion we agreed that we needed to be there and it was there that God worked out Tom's salvation in the most unusual and extraordinary way. As soon as Tom arrived, and introductions had been made, Tom went on to tell Frank he was also here because he needed major surgery for his heart. My husband immediately asked Tom if he could pray for him. "Yes, please do, responded Tom." "Before I do Tom, said Frank, have you ever received the Lord Jesus as your Savior?" OH MY , this is incredible!! The man who refused all those years to hear anything about the Lord, without hesitation said, "no, how do I do that?" How ironic! My new husband Frank led my ex husband Tom in a salvation prayer and prayed also for his upcoming surgery which went very well. All Tom's visits here since then always include getting in touch with us. We have had him over to our house and he actually says "it is an honor to come here" Look at how God can change a heart!

Frank and I continue to pray a prayer of thanksgiving for all He has done for us, especially our marriage... a gift beyond expectation. Together we honor and serve the Lord through our healing and prayer ministry at, Village of Faith Church, in Farmingville, New York. God has led us to it and He continues to walk us through it.

So now that you've heard my story, and you know who God is, why it's important to know the Word, stand in faith, speak with wisdom, and wait on the Lord, are you fully persuaded no obstacle is too big to overcome?

Are you persuaded that God is who He says He is, faithful and true? That you are who God says you are... beloved, accepted, righteous, forgiven, and victorious?

Are you persuaded that to submit to God in obedience brings blessings? That trials are not from God, but that He's there with you, strengthening you through them?

Are you persuaded that prayer and praise are two powerful weapons to use against the enemy?

Are you persuaded that the wisdom of God is the will of God and when you use His wisdom, you'll be on the right path doing the right thing?

Are you persuaded that His grace will empower you and His peace will keep you? That you have a great hope to hold onto?

Are you persuaded that when you build on the right foundation, His truth, you will be stable, secure, and steadfast?

If your answer is "yes," then I'm happy to say, you are now equipped for your own journey... *from* Wimp to Warrior.

Author's Note

Is there anyone who isn't sure of their salvation? That one day heaven will be your home? The word of God says, *if you believe in your heart and confess with your mouth that Jesus died and rose again you will be saved* (Romans 10:9 NIV).

Salvation is the most wonderful gift you will ever receive. It's a free gift and when you receive it, God's spirit comes to live in you, filling you and working in and for you to become all that He has planned for you.

If you want to be certain of your salvation, simply pray this prayer:

Father, I believe that Jesus died and that He rose again. I ask You to forgive all my sins. Fill me with your Spirit and help me, from this day forward, to live a victorious life, guided and directed by You. Thank You for saving me and giving me the gift of eternal life.

I ask this all in the name of Jesus. *Amen*

Susan Karas is an inspirational writer whose true stories have touched hearts and encouraged many smiles. She is a frequent contributor to *Guideposts* magazines, *Chicken Soup for the Soul* books, *Marriage Partnership*, and *Christian Life Times*. For more information contact: suezfoofer@aol.com

CPSIA information can be obtained at www.ICGtesting.com
Printed in the USA
BVOW072057100413

317855BV00003B/289/P